LEADER GUID

RESTING IN THE SHADOW OF THE **ALMIGHTY**

AMY BYRD + BECKY DEDGE

LifeWay Press®
Nashville, Tennessee

ISBN: 978-1-4300-3978-5
Item Number: 005720742

Dewey Decimal Classification Number: 248.83
Subject Heading: GIRLS \ BIBLE. O.T. PSALMS 91 \ FAITH \ SPIRITUAL LIFE

Printed in the United States of America

We believe that the Bible has God for its author; salvation for its end; and truth, without any mixture of error, for its matter and that all Scripture is totally true and trustworthy. To review LifeWay's doctrinal guideline, please visit
www.lifeway.com/doctrinalguideline.

Student Ministry Publishing
LifeWay Church Resources
One LifeWay Plaza
Nashville, TN 37234-0144

Table of Contents

SPECIAL THANKS 4

ABOUT THE AUTHORS 5

HOW TO USE 6

SESSION ONE: MADE TO DWELL 7

SESSION TWO: DWELLING DISTRACTIONS 12

SESSION THREE: DWELLING IN COMMUNITY 17

SESSION FOUR: DWELLING DELIGHTS 22

SESSION FIVE: YOUR DWELLING PLACE 27

SESSION SIX: FAITHFUL PROTECTOR 32

SESSION SEVEN: A SAFE DWELLING 37

SESSION EIGHT: THE PROMISE 42

Special Thanks

WE ARE ESPECIALLY GRATEFUL TO...

Our husbands for loving and encouraging us through this season full of late night writing. We love you!

Our dear friends for praying for us, reading through drafts, and keeping us laughing. We love you!

Our families for supporting us and pointing us to Jesus, our true dwelling place! We love you!

Our friends at LifeWay who embraced our vision and partnered with us to bring this study to life! We love you!

Our One True joy and satisfaction...Jesus! You are so good to us! We agape you!

Soli Deo Gloria

Amy & Becky

About the Authors

AMY BYRD

Amy has a desire to make much of Jesus and loves all things student ministry. She has the joy to serve as the Director of Girls Ministry at Hunter Street Baptist Church in Birmingham, AL. Amy loves spending time with her husband, William, and her family and dear friends. In addition to her role at HSBC, Amy also serves on the leadership team for LifeWay Girls Ministry. Her ultimate desire is to see girls know their worth as daughters of the Most High and know Him as their Savior.

BECKY DEDGE

Becky longs to see girls love Jesus and know their identity and satisfaction is in Christ, not the world. The Lord has allowed her to serve in student ministry for a little over 10 years. Becky is currently on staff with Hunter Street Baptist Church Student Ministry in Birmingham, AL. It is here that she lives with her husband and 2 year old son. God has been so gracious, and she is thankful to be a part of His work.

How to Use

This Leader Guide is designed to help you plan and facilitate weekly group gatherings. There is a separate student book (Item #: 005720741) which includes personal study pages that participants will use to dig into Scripture and dwell on specific truths related to each week's focus. Your group gatherings should be a time when girls can discuss what they studied the previous week, dig deeper into God's Word, and be challenged to memorize Scripture and apply it to their daily lives.

THE GOAL OF THIS STUDY

In the first four sessions, we will examine what it means to dwell on the Word of God, in the presence of God, and with the people of God. Through the last four sessions, we will dwell on Psalm 91 and experience the joy of resting in the shadow of the Almighty.

THE STRUCTURE OF THIS STUDY

Each group time will include the following elements:

* **GET STARTED...** This section is designed to give you ideas for opening activities that illustrate a specific truth or theme related to each week's content. These activities will also help you create an environment conducive to group participation.
* **TALK IT OUT...** This portion of the session will be used to review what girls studied over the past week and give them an opportunity to share anything they highlighted in the student book or had questions about. You will find a *Quick Review* outline in this section that references the main points of the personal study pages from the previous week. You will also find discussion questions to help guide this weekly review.
* **FURTHER STUDY...** This section will give you additional Scripture and discussion questions to challenge your group to go deeper in their understanding of each week's theme.
* **LIVE IT OUT...** This section focuses on application and encourages participants to consider steps they need to take as they move forward.
* **DWELL CHALLENGE...** As you close out each group session, you'll find two challenges listed here. One is called *In This Together*. Use this time to build community and encourage accountability. The second is called *Dwell on This.* During this time, encourage girls to share how each week's focal passage has impacted their lives.

Made to Dwell

I AM THE VINE; YOU ARE THE BRANCHES.
THE ONE WHO REMAINS IN ME AND I IN HIM
PRODUCES MUCH FRUIT, BECAUSE YOU CAN
DO NOTHING WITHOUT ME.

JOHN 15:5

Get Started

Since this is your first meeting together as a small group, help your girls get to know each other. Consider leading them in some version of a name game or get-to-know-you game. Here are a few ideas.

Option One (younger girls): Pass the Candy

Bring a bag of candy like M&M's® or Skittles®. Pass the bag around the circle and encourage girls to get as many pieces as they would like but to wait until everyone has some before eating. Once the bag has made its way around, inform girls that you would like them to share about themselves based on the candy they are holding. Assign each color of candy a different fact such as red=most embarrassing moment, yellow=happiest memory from childhood, green=most adventurous thing you've ever done, etc. Allow girls to go around the circle several times and share whatever fact(s) their candy relates to.

Option Two (older girls): The Question Game

Before the session, write a variety of questions on a sheet of paper. Tear the paper so that each strip has only one question. Place questions in a hat and allow each girl to draw a strip of paper and answer the question listed. Consider using a variety of questions with some silly or light hearted and others more serious or spiritual in nature. Examples could include: Who is one person from history you would like to spend the day with? If you were given the opportunity to travel for a month, where would you go? If you could change one thing about the world, what would you change?

Transition: Encourage girls to enjoy getting to know each other better over the next eight weeks. Challenge them to make this time together a priority and to stay connected during the days between group meetings. Set the tone for how you want girls to interact with one another in these group times, and help them understand how important it will be for them to honor one another as they begin to open up about spiritual matters.

Talk it Out

Review the material the girls studied last week. Encourage them to share anything they highlighted in the student book or had questions about.

>>QUICK SUMMARY:

1   We were created in the image of God and made to dwell in His presence.

2   When sin entered the world, our fellowship with God was broken. Because of the fall, we are born in a sinful state and deserve death.

3   Jesus came to die for our sins and reconcile us back to God.

4   Only through Christ can we draw near to God and find our true dwelling place.

Once girls have shared highlights, lead them to discuss the following questions to ensure they understand the main points for this week. These three questions are listed in the student book at the top of page 20. Every session will have a **Dwelling Together** page at the end which will be used in this group time. Encourage girls to turn to this page and follow along during the group meeting.

* How is your daily life different when you dwell with Christ?
* Describe the results of trying to find fulfillment in people and places other than Christ.
* In what ways were we made to dwell?

Further Study

It's very likely that not every member of your group has experienced salvation, so make the gospel message the starting point for this study. If they read Session One this week, they have already been exposed to the good news of Jesus Christ several times. Ensure that they understand the message of the gospel and make note of anyone who seems to be unsure so you can follow up with her later.

Encourage them to discuss the following as a group:

* What makes the gospel message different from every other religion? (Jesus became a man but remained perfect. He then gave Himself up for us as a sacrifice, defeated death, and is alive today. We are the only ones who serve a living God!)

* What does it mean to surrender your life to Christ? (It means to submit to the lordship of Christ and trust that His work on the cross is enough to save you from sin.)

Help girls define the following words:
- Atonement* = the work Christ did in His life and death to earn our salvation
- Repentance* = a heartfelt sorrow for sin, a renouncing of it, and a sincere commitment to forsake it and walk in obedience to Christ
- Faith* = trust or dependence on God

  *Wayne Grudem, Bible Doctrine (Grand Rapids, MI: Zondervan, 1999).

In this week's study, the girls were challenged to identify their current dwelling place—where they go for rest, comfort, and security. Dig a little deeper and challenge your girls to be honest as they discuss the following:

* How do you feel when you are in the place or with the person you consider your refuge?
* Why do you run to that particular place or person?
* Why do you think it is easier to choose an earthly refuge rather than make our constant dwelling place with Christ? What are the dangers of making an earthly refuge our first choice?

We want girls to see that they were made to dwell in Christ. Nothing in this world will ever fully bring rest, comfort, and security to our souls except Him.

INVITE A MEMBER OF YOUR GROUP TO READ JOHN 15:1-8.

This is a beautiful picture of what it means to dwell in Christ. Help your girls see how Christ is the vine and each of us are the branches. Allow them to point out anything in these verses that stands out to them.

Discuss the following:
* Where does this passage say we, as the branches, should remain?
* What happens when a branch remains in the vine?
* Can a branch produce fruit away from the vine? Explain.
* What does it mean to bear fruit?

When believers dwell in Christ, we receive the nourishment we need to bear spiritual fruit. But, when we choose to dwell in this world, we wither and remain fruitless.

Challenge your girls to examine their lives as you ask the following:
* Are you connected to the Vine? Are you spending time in God's Word and in prayer daily? Explain.
* Are you bearing spiritual fruit or are you withering? Explain.

Allow your girls a few minutes to consider what they have learned in this session and how it applies to their lives. Direct them to page 20 in their student books and encourage them to answer the following questions in the space provided.

* **What has God revealed to you this week about the places or people you run to for refuge?**
* **What changes do you need to make?**

Once girls have recorded their answers, challenge them to follow through with any changes they listed. One way the girls will help each other follow through is by encouraging and praying for one another. Transition to the Dwell Challenge.

Dwell Challenge

Each session will conclude with a time of prayer, accountability, and Scripture memory.

IN THIS TOGETHER: Instruct girls to find a partner or a small group of three and share what they wrote in the *Live It Out* section on page 20 of the student book. Point them to the box called *In This Together* where they can list each other's prayer requests. They can also make notes to help encourage and hold one another accountable to follow through with anything God is leading them to live out this week.

DWELL ON THIS: Direct girls to remain with their partners/groups from the previous activity and encourage them to consider how this week's focal verse, John 15:5, has impacted their lives. Invite each girl to share how God is using the truths of this verse to shape her perspective and character.

Close your time in prayer.

NOTE: Make sure girls know that you are available to talk if they have questions about salvation or anything else discussed in your group time. Be faithful to follow up and have a conversation with them about their relationship with Christ.

Dwelling Distractions

NO TEMPTATION HAS OVERTAKEN YOU EXCEPT WHAT IS COMMON TO HUMANITY. GOD IS FAITHFUL, AND HE WILL NOT ALLOW YOU TO BE TEMPTED BEYOND WHAT YOU ARE ABLE, BUT WITH THE TEMPTATION HE WILL ALSO PROVIDE A WAY OF ESCAPE SO THAT YOU ARE ABLE TO BEAR IT.

1 CORINTHIANS 10:13

Get Started

This past week of study included some difficult realities as we focused on spiritual distractions and idols in our lives. This group session has the potential to be deep and effective if your girls are willing to open up. As you guide them through the discussion, consider sharing a few examples from your own spiritual journey that will allow them to see how God has helped you focus on Him and deal with idols along the way. Get things started with one of the following options.

Option One (younger girls):
Pass out a note card and pen to each of your girls. Guide them to write the answer to the question below as you read it aloud:

> ✻ **What are the top five priorities in your life right now (things or activities you put at the top of your list no matter what)?**

Transition: After giving them time to answer, allow girls to share their thoughts. Encourage them to circle any of the five priorities they listed that have eternal significance (anything that glorifies God and draws them closer to Him). Some of the girls may have put God first on their lists, while others may not have thought about the question from a spiritual perspective. Graciously challenge the group to recognize how easy it is to put earthly things and activities (even good ones) before our relationship with God.

Option Two (older girls):
Encourage girls to sit in a circle on the floor. Open with prayer, then lead them to discuss the following questions:

> ✻ **What were your initial thoughts as you studied about idols and sin this past week?**
> ✻ **Is it hard for you to be honest with yourself and others about the sin that you struggle with? Why or why not?**
> ✻ **What idol(s) did you identify as you went through the study?**

Challenge them to discuss the evidence of sin they see in their own lives. Point out that the beauty of this small group environment is that they can be honest with one another and help hold each other accountable in areas of struggle. This also means they are being trusted to keep what is shared within the group confidential.

Transition: Challenge girls to recognize that we all have areas of weakness that make us vulnerable to the enemy's temptations. His goal is to keep us focused on the things of this world. But the Lord graciously offers us the power and wisdom to stay focused on Him.

Talk it Out

Review the material the girls studied last week. Encourage them to share anything they highlighted in the student book or had questions about.

>>QUICK SUMMARY:

1   We can be easily distracted by the things of the world.
2   Anything in our lives that we prioritize above God is an idol.
3   We must identify the idols in our lives and call on God to help us flee from temptation.
4   When we fail, God offers forgiveness and draws our hearts back to Him.

Once girls have shared highlights, lead them to discuss the following questions to ensure they understand the main points for this week. These three questions are listed in the student book at the top of page 34. Every session will have a **Dwelling Together** page at the end which will be used in this group time. Encourage girls to turn to this page and follow along during the group meeting.

  * **Why do you think we are so easily distracted by the things of this world?**
  * **In what ways does God's grace and forgiveness bring us freedom?**
  * **How has dwelling on Jesus this week (or other times) affected your thoughts and actions?**

Further Study

On page 29 of the student book, girls were challenged to read John 10:10 and compare the enemy's ultimate goal with what Jesus offers us. Lead them to share what they wrote in that section.

Remind girls that the thief wants to kill, steal, and destroy. Encourage them to share about times when they have sensed the enemy trying to steal their joy, destroy their reputation, or discourage them spiritually in one way or another.

Now, point girls to the reality that Jesus stands victorious over the enemy and offers us abundant life. Encourage them to share how they have found victory over specific temptations and a sense of joy through their relationship with Christ.

Take this opportunity to share how you have experienced abundant life in Christ. Help students see that this fullness of life comes only when we seek joy, satisfaction, and protection in Christ alone. When we attempt to live in our own power and fight in our own strength, we grow weary and feel like we are merely surviving instead of living abundantly.

At the end of this past week's study, girls were encouraged to read Philippians 4:8 and identify how they could keep from being so easily distracted by the things of this world. Let's dig a little deeper into Philippians 4 and discover more truths to help us stay focused on Jesus.

INVITE A MEMBER OF YOUR GROUP TO READ PHILIPPIANS 4:4-8.

In this passage, the apostle Paul calls believers in Philippi to embrace a life of joy, grace, and peace. This spiritually fulfilling and effective life can only be found in Christ. When we live in the manner Paul describes, spiritual distractions are minimized as Christ is glorified. The enemy will never stop trying to tempt us as long as we are alive, but there is victory when we keep our minds fixed firmly on Jesus.

Discuss the following:
* **What does it mean to rejoice?**
* **How does rejoicing impact our attitude and perspective?**
* **How should we deal with worry and anxiousness according to this passage?**
* **What does verse seven say about the peace of God?**
* **Encourage your group to share examples of how focusing on Christ has given them peace even in difficult circumstances. Be prepared to share examples from your own life.**

Refer back to the **Consider This** box on page 24 of the student book. Remind girls of what the word *worry* meant in this passage. "In Luke 10:41, when Jesus pointed out to Martha that she was 'worried' about many things, He used a Greek word meaning anxious, distracted, drawn apart. He was painting a picture for her that she was letting earthly distractions draw her away from what was most important—dwelling in His presence."
James Strong, *The New Strong's Expanded Exhaustive Concordance of the Bible* (Nashville, TN: Thomas Nelson, 2010). Available from the Internet: *www.biblehub.com*

Challenge your girls to examine their lives as you ask the following:
* **Are you often worried or anxious about things? How does that affect your spiritual life?**
* **Are you willing to rejoice, pray, and give thanks to God in every circumstance? Why or why not?**

Live it Out

Allow your girls a few minutes to consider what they have learned in this session and how it applies to their lives. Direct them to page 34 in their student books and encourage them to answer the following questions in the space provided.

* **What most often distracts you from dwelling in God's presence?**
* **Are there areas of vulnerability in your life where you need to develop accountability? If so, what steps do you need to take to develop accountability in these areas?**

Once girls have recorded their answers, challenge them to follow through with any changes they listed. One way the girls will help each other follow through is by encouraging and praying for one another. Transition to the Dwell Challenge.

Dwell Challenge

Each session will conclude with a time of prayer and accountability groups.

IN THIS TOGETHER: Instruct girls to find a partner or a small group of three and share what they wrote in the *Live It Out* section on page 34 of the student book. Point them to the box called *In This Together* where they can list each other's prayer requests. They can also make notes to help encourage and hold one another accountable to follow through with anything God is leading them to live out this week.

DWELL ON THIS: Direct girls to remain with their partners/groups from the previous activity and encourage them to consider how this week's focal verse, 1 Corinthians 10:13, has impacted their lives. Invite each girl to share how God is using the truths of this verse to shape her perspective and character.

Close your time in prayer.

Dwelling in Community

AND LET US BE CONCERNED ABOUT ONE ANOTHER IN ORDER TO PROMOTE LOVE AND GOOD WORKS, NOT STAYING AWAY FROM OUR WORSHIP MEETINGS, AS SOME HABITUALLY DO, BUT ENCOURAGING EACH OTHER, AND ALL THE MORE AS YOU SEE THE DAY DRAWING NEAR.

HEBREWS 10:24-25

Get Started

Use this time together to reinforce the truths your girls have studied this past week about the importance of community. Help them see how precious these moments of laughter, prayer, learning, and encouragement can be.

Instruct girls to line up and face you. Inform them that you are going to call out various statements. If they can identify with a statement, they should step forward. Once each round is over they can return to a straight line until the next statement. Below are some examples to get you started (you can add to these or change them). We recommend you start with a few fun or lighthearted ones so they will feel more comfortable stepping forward. Let them know that the statements will get more serious as the game progresses.

Step forward if...
* You have ever tripped and embarrassed yourself in front of people.
* You have ever stayed up all night reading a book or watching movies.
* You have ever traveled out of the country.
* You have ever lost something that was really important to you.
* You have ever been upset with your parents.
* You have ever said something you wished you could take back.
* You have ever felt alone.
* You have ever asked someone to forgive you for something you did.
* You have ever felt betrayed by a friend.
* You have ever struggled with a sin.
* You have ever lost someone you loved.

Transition: Our backgrounds, families, and circumstances are all different, yet many of our experiences in life are similar. Sometimes we feel like we are the only ones who struggle, fail, or face difficult situations. We shy away from letting others in because we don't think they will understand our thoughts and emotions. In reality, we weren't wired to face this life on our own, we were created for community. We need people to stand with us through the ups and downs of life. We need people who will point us to Jesus and remind us of His unfailing love no matter what we face. We need to laugh and celebrate good times together, we need encouragement in the difficult times, and we need accountability as we live our lives for God's glory.

Talk it Out

Review the material the girls studied last week. Encourage them to share anything they highlighted in the student book or had questions about.

>>QUICK SUMMARY:

1   The Lord desires for us to experience biblical community.
2   Who we spend time with matters.
3   God has uniquely designed us to serve Him within a local church body.
4   Within the church, we should be challenging and encouraging one another spiritually.

Once girls have shared highlights, lead them to discuss the following questions to ensure they understand the main points for this week. These three questions are listed in the student book at the top of page 48. Every session will have a *Dwelling Together* page at the end which will be used in this group time. Encourage girls to turn to this page and follow along during the group meeting.

* **Describe biblical community.**
* **Why is unity within the church so important?**
* **How have the people in your church body encouraged and challenged you spiritually?**

Further Study

Lead your girls to share how many friends or followers they have on social media. Ask them if they know all of those friends/followers really well? The reality is they probably don't know all of them well. Help them see how easily social media can give us a false sense of community. God desires for His children to experience real connections and biblical community.

INVITE SEVERAL GIRLS TO READ EPHESIANS 4:1-16.

Discuss the following:

* **What does it mean to walk worthy of the calling you have received?**
* **What is the source of our unity as believers?**
* **Why do you think unity within the church is so difficult to maintain?**
* **For what purpose has the Lord given us spiritual gifts (vv. 11-12)?**
* **What does it mean to speak the truth in love?**

Challenge your girls to examine their lives as you ask the following:
  * **Do your words and actions point people to Jesus? Explain.**
  * **Are you a person that strives for unity and builds others up? Why or why not?**

In light of this passage in Ephesians and other passages your girls have studied this week, help them understand biblical community more fully by discussing the following.

Relationships with Lost People: It's likely that some of your girls have questions about friendships with those who are not believers. They may be wondering if the concept of biblical community requires that they completely cut off the people in their lives who don't know Christ. Help them understand that biblical community should actually compel us to interact with unbelievers so that we can share the gospel with them. When we are closely connected to the body of Christ and dwelling deeply in God's Word, then our hearts will sense when the Lord is leading us to spend time with those who are lost. As we are living with this missional mindset, we must stay in community with other believers who can pray for us, encourage us, and hold us accountable if we lose sight of our eternal goal. Refer back to page 42 in the student book for more Scripture and context on this issue.

Iron Sharpening Iron: Help your girls understand that we are all at different levels of maturity in our faith and we need each other as we grow. We need people to pour into our lives and sharpen us with their words and actions. We also need to actively seek opportunities to disciple those who are younger in the faith.

Serving the Church: On pages 43-44, girls were challenged to consider how they are currently serving within their church. It might be helpful for your girls to take a spiritual gifts test during your small group time or encourage them to take it during the week and come prepared to share the results. This will help them identify ways they can most effectively serve the church. If your church does not have a spiritual gifts test available, you can find one online: *www.lifeway.com/lwc/files/lwcF_PDF_Discover_Your_Spiritual_Gifts.pdf*

Connecting with a Local Church: The girls in your group are most likely already members of your church, but it is important to help them know what to look for when joining a fellowship of believers, as they may move to a new city one day or go away for college. What church they join will matter. Help them understand the importance of seeking out a church that is gospel-centered, mission-minded, compassionate, and grounded in God's Word.

Live it Out

Allow your girls a few minutes to consider what they have learned in this session and how it applies to their lives. Direct them to page 48 in their student books and encourage them to answer the following questions in the space provided.

* ✷ **Do you willingly share your life with other believers or do you hold back parts of your heart? Explain.**
* ✷ **Based on what you've learned this week, how has your view of church changed? What do you need to do to be more fully involved in biblical community?**

Once girls have recorded their answers, challenge them to follow through with any changes they listed. One way the girls will help each other follow through is by encouraging and praying for one another. Transition to the Dwell Challenge.

Dwell Challenge

Each session will conclude with a time of prayer and accountability groups.

IN THIS TOGETHER: Instruct girls to find a partner or a small group of three and share what they wrote in the *Live It Out* section on page 48 of the student book. Point them to the box called *In This Together* where they can list each other's prayer requests. They can also make notes to help encourage and hold one another accountable to follow through with anything God is leading them to live out this week.

DWELL ON THIS: Direct girls to remain with their partners/groups from the previous activity and encourage them to consider how this week's focal verses, Hebrews 10:24-25, have impacted their lives. Invite each girl to share how God is using the truths of these verses to shape her perspective and character.

Challenge girls to contact those in their group several times this week to pray together or just to encourage one another.

Close your time in prayer.

Dwelling Delights

I AM AT REST IN GOD ALONE;
MY SALVATION COMES FROM HIM. HE ALONE IS MY
ROCK AND MY SALVATION, MY STRONGHOLD;
I WILL NEVER BE SHAKEN.

PSALM 62:1-2

Get Started

Even with a title that includes the word "delights," we know this was not an easy week of study. It can be difficult to think about the conditions we have placed on our lives and how those affect our true delight in Christ. To be honest about the deepest longings of our hearts requires prayer, encouragement, and a safe place to process. We hope this weekly gathering has become a sweet refuge where your girls are learning how to dwell together in God's Word and in His presence.

Lead your girls to stand on one side of the room. Explain to the group that their goal is to get safely to the other side of the room. At first this will seem like a really easy assignment. But before you say "go," give them one or more conditions they must follow, such as:

* They must get to the other side while blindfolded.
* They must get to the other side with everyone in the group attached at the ankle. (Use bandanas or something soft to connect them.)
* They must get to the other side with their eyes closed and walking backward.
* They must all get to the other side but only two people can touch the ground.

You get the picture! Once they have made it to the other side (or time has been called), invite them to sit down and share about the experience. Ask if the activity was more difficult than they first thought it would be when they heard the initial instructions. Help them see that the original task was uncomplicated until conditions were given and their preconceived notions of how the task would be accomplished were altered.

Transition: Conditions are set as a way of restricting or modifying original plans. When we place conditions on our tasks or relationships, we are indicating that there are limits to what we will do unless our specific requirements are met. We probably do this more often than we realize, even placing conditions on our spiritual growth.

Refer girls back to David Livingstone's prayer on page 59 of the student book. Allow them to share their thoughts about his words and what kind of conditions they might place after each line of that prayer.

Lord, send me anywhere...
Lay any burden on me...
Severe any ties...

Help girls to recognize that our conditions prevent us from fully trusting and delighting in God.

Talk it Out

Review the material the girls studied last week. Encourage them to share anything they highlighted in the student book or had questions about.

>>QUICK SUMMARY:

1   Only in Christ can we find what our souls long for.
2   Only God can give us true satisfaction and joy.
3   Only God can offer unwavering hope.
4   To delight in God is to trust Him and surrender to His will.

Once girls have shared highlights, lead them to discuss the following questions to ensure they understand the main points for this week. These three questions are listed in the student book at the top of page 62. Every session will have a **Dwelling Together** page at the end which will be used in this group time. Encourage girls to turn to this page and follow along during the group meeting.

* **What do you think keeps us from enjoying the presence of God? Fear? Uncertainty? Busyness?**
* **How is joy different from happiness?**
* **If we say we trust God, why do we struggle to surrender our hopes and dreams to Him?**

Further Study

It can be challenging in this broken world to really understand how to experience joy, satisfaction, hope, and trust in the Lord. Often, our circumstances leave us with more questions than answers. Ask your girls if they can relate to any of these questions:

* **How can I be joyful when my family is falling apart?**
* **Why does God let tragedy strike those who love and trust Him?**
* **How can I feel joyful after losing someone I love?**
* **Why should I be hopeful when all my plans and dreams have fallen apart?**

These are difficult questions. And we may never get the answers we seek, or at least not the answers we want. But even when our families are broken, our lives are a mess, and our dreams are unfulfilled, there is still a way to find deep satisfaction for our souls. We can delight in Christ no matter what circumstances we are facing.

INVITE A MEMBER OF YOUR GROUP TO READ <u>PSALM 37:3-6.</u>

Discuss the following:
* What commands are we given in this passage?
* Does verse 4 mean that we can ask God for anything and He will give it to us? Explain.
* In what ways are trust, obedience, and delight connected to one another?
* What does it mean to commit your way to the Lord?
* What promise is given to those who commit their lives to the Lord?

This passage is packed with beautiful truths that help us understand what it looks like to delight in the Lord. It starts with trust that moves us to obedience which leads to delight. This delight comes from enjoying the presence of the Lord through consistent fellowship. When we fix our eyes on His grace and glory, our hearts are stirred by His plans and purposes. The end result is that our deepest desires fall in sync with God's desires for us. The more we delight in Him, the more we desire to bring Him glory. The more we bring Him glory, the more we discover that He is our greatest delight.

Challenge your girls to examine their lives as you ask the following:
* Do you trust God with your life? Why or why not?
* How have you seen God honor your obedience and commitment to Him?

Allow your girls a few minutes to consider what they have learned in this session and how it applies to their lives. Direct them to page 62 in their student books and encourage them to answer the following questions in the space provided.

* Based on what you've learned this week, how will you approach hardships differently from now on?
* Who or what is currently the desire of your heart? Is it Jesus or are you trying to find satisfaction elsewhere? What changes do you need to make?

Once girls have recorded their answers, challenge them to follow through with any changes they listed. One way the girls will help each other follow through is by encouraging and praying for one another. Transition to the Dwell Challenge.

Dwell Challenge

Each session will conclude with a time of prayer and accountability groups.

IN THIS TOGETHER: Instruct girls to find a partner or a small group of three and share what they wrote in the *Live It Out* section on page 62 of the student book. Point them to the box called *In This Together* where they can list each other's prayer requests. They can also make notes to help encourage and hold one another accountable to follow through with anything God is leading them to live out this week.

DWELL ON THIS: Direct girls to remain with their partners/groups from the previous activity and encourage them to consider how this week's focal verses, Psalm 62:1-2, have impacted their lives. Invite each girl to share how God is using the truths of these verses to shape her perspective and character.

Close your time in prayer.

Your Dwelling Place

THE ONE WHO LIVES UNDER THE PROTECTION
OF THE MOST HIGH DWELLS IN THE SHADOW
OF THE ALMIGHTY.

PSALM 91:1

This week we moved from a broad overview of dwelling to a more focused look at one specific passage of Scripture. We will continue to dig into Psalm 91 for the remainder of this study. Our prayer is that as girls begin to practice what it means to dwell on God's Word, they will discover the life-changing joy of His presence. We hope this study stirs in every girl a passion for Scripture that will continue throughout their lives.

Option One (younger girls):

Most of us have played the game "hide-and-go-seek" at some point in our lives. Ask girls if they can remember playing that game as a child. Did they have a perfect hiding place where no one could find them? What made that spot such a great hiding place? Guide them to think about this season of their lives, and ask if they have a place (or places) now where they like to go to get away from noise or stress (or to hide from a sibling). Ask how they went about choosing that particular place and how often they spend time there.

Transition: What makes a good hiding place is a sense of safety and some kind of barrier between us and whatever "enemy" we are hiding from. Spiritually speaking, we can't hide from our greatest enemy, but we can find safety and protection in the presence of God Almighty. We will continue to look at what God's protection means for our lives in this session.

Option Two (older girls):

Lead girls to discuss the significance of trust in each of the following scenarios:

* Success of a sports team
* Safety of emergency personnel working together (firemen, policemen, military, etc.)
* Health of relationships (family, friendships, boyfriend)
* Unity of this Bible study group
* Our relationship with God

Transition: Ask girls why trust is hard in some situations. Encourage them to share examples of how their willingness to trust has grown because of particular people or circumstances. They probably all recognize the importance of trusting others and being a trustworthy person. But have they considered how much trust impacts their relationship with God? Challenge them to ponder that question for a moment before you move on.

Talk it Out

Review the material the girls studied last week. Encourage them to share anything they highlighted in the student book or had questions about.

>>QUICK SUMMARY:

1   We must learn to dwell in the presence of God consistently.
2   The Lord is our protector and our hiding place.
3   We have been invited to rest in the shadow of the Almighty.
4   God is a refuge and fortress that we can fully trust.

Once girls have shared highlights, lead them to discuss the following questions to ensure they understand the main points for this week. These three questions are listed in the student book at the top of page 74. Every session will have a **Dwelling Together** page at the end which will be used in this group time. Encourage girls to turn to this page and follow along during the group meeting.

* **By nature we strive for independence, yet God calls us to be fully dependent on Him. Why is dependence on God so necessary?**
* **What does it mean to rest in the shadow of the Almighty on a daily basis?**
* **In what ways does dwelling on God's Word bring peace to any circumstance?**

Further Study

One of the key points from this session is centered on trusting God. The degree to which we trust God affects our obedience, our peace, and our fellowship with Him.

Start off by discussing the following question:

* **Why do you think people struggle to trust God?**

Encourage girls to share about times they have struggled to trust God. Be prepared to share your own experiences and how God has deepened your trust through the ups and downs of life.

Often people struggle to trust God because they don't know enough about His character to recognize that He is completely trustworthy. Help your girls discover more about the character of God by looking at what Scripture has to say.

Divide your girls into three groups and assign each group one of the following passages. Instruct them to read the passage and make note of what these verses reveal about the character of God.

GROUP ONE: READ PSALM 9:7-10.
GROUP TWO: READ PSALM 28:6-8.
GROUP THREE: READ PSALM 40:3-5.

After a few minutes, bring the girls back together. Allow each group to read their assigned passage and share their thoughts. Discuss how we should respond to God in light of His trustworthy character.

We can trust God because He is perfectly faithful. He is just, righteous and good. The more intimately we know God, the deeper our trust in Him will be. And the more we trust Him, the easier it will be to rest in Him.

Discuss the following:
* **How important is rest to our physical health? What happens when we don't get enough rest?**
* **How is spiritual rest similar to physical rest?**

Help girls see how rest and trust are connected. Ask girls to describe the ideal environment (sounds, lighting, temperature) they need to physically rest. Though our preferences may be different, we all need to feel a certain sense of safety in order to let our defenses down and really rest. There must be some level of trust that our situation is secure in order for our minds and bodies to drift into the kind of physical rest that refreshes us. The same is true in our spiritual lives—in order for us to truly rest in the shadow of the Almighty, we must trust in His character. That's why worry and exhaustion are often signs that we are struggling to trust God in some area of our lives.

Challenge your girls to examine their lives as you ask the following:
* **Do you trust God more than you trust yourself? More than you trust those closest to you? Explain.**

We encourage you to end this time by playing the song "Oceans" by Hillsong (*Zion*, Hillsong, 2013). Invite girls to listen closely and think carefully about the message of the song.

Live it Out

Allow your girls a few minutes to consider what they have learned in this session and how it applies to their lives. Direct them to page 74 in their student books and encourage them to answer the following questions in the space provided.

* **In what areas of your life do you need to more fully trust and depend on God?**
* **God wants to accomplish eternally significant things in and through you. What is keeping you from stepping out in faith and following His lead?**

Once girls have recorded their answers, challenge them to follow through with any changes they listed. One way the girls will help each other follow through is by encouraging and praying for one another. Transition to the Dwell Challenge.

Dwell Challenge

Each session will conclude with a time of prayer and accountability groups.

IN THIS TOGETHER: Instruct girls to find a partner or a small group of three and share what they wrote in the *Live It Out* section on page 74 of the student book. Point them to the box called *In This Together* where they can list each other's prayer requests. They can also make notes to help encourage and hold one another accountable to follow through with anything God is leading them to live out this week.

DWELL ON THIS: Direct girls to remain with their partners/groups from the previous activity and encourage them to consider how this week's focal verse, Psalm 91:1, has impacted their lives. Invite each girl to share how God is using the truths of this verse to shape her perspective and character.

Challenge them to contact those in their group several times this week to pray together or just to encourage one another.

Close your time in prayer.

Faithful Protector

HE WILL COVER YOU WITH HIS FEATHERS;
YOU WILL TAKE REFUGE UNDER HIS WINGS.
HIS FAITHFULNESS WILL BE A PROTECTIVE SHIELD.

PSALM 91:4

Get Started

We hope this journey through Psalm 91 has been a blessing to you as you have read and prepared each week to lead your girls. This past week focused on God's faithfulness and challenged us to stay alert as we face spiritual warfare.

Psalm 91:4 has been a verse of encouragement and inspiration for us throughout the process of writing this resource. Read this verse to your girls and challenge them to think about the picture it paints of God's protective nature and affection for His children.

> "He will cover you with His feathers; you will take refuge under His wings.
> His faithfulness will be a protective shield."
> Psalm 91:4

Provide poster board or large sheets of paper and markers. Divide your girls into two groups. Instruct each group to work together to create a visual representation of this verse. Encourage them to create it in such a way that each phrase of the verse is represented.

Transition: Allow each group to share their creative work with the others. Encourage girls to discuss what this verse says about the character of God. Lead them to consider how we should respond to God's protective nature and affection for us.

Talk it Out

Review the material the girls studied last week. Encourage them to share anything they highlighted in the student book or had questions about.

>>QUICK SUMMARY:

1. The enemy wants us to fall into temptation and be drawn away from the Lord.
2. We will always struggle with temptation to sin.
3. With God's strength, we can flee and find victory over sin.
4. God is our faithful protector.

Once girls have shared highlights, lead them to discuss the following questions to ensure they understand the main points for this week. These three questions are listed in the student book at the top of page 86. Every session will have a *Dwelling Together* page at the end which will be used in this group time. Encourage girls to turn to this page and follow along during the group meeting.

* What does Psalm 91 say about the protective nature of God?
* What is spiritual warfare and how does it affect us?
* How can we stand and fight against our enemy?

Further Study

Dig in and help your girls discover how the Lord protects and defends His children against the plots of the enemy!

INVITE A MEMBER OF YOUR GROUP TO READ JOHN 10:11-15.

Ask girls if they know anything about sheep. Here are some random facts that you can share.
1   Sheep are dumb.
2   Sheep do not know how or when to lay down to rest.
3   Sheep do not know how to find food on their own.
4   Sheep NEED a shepherd.

Let's break down this passage together and have the girls apply the truths found in these verses to their own lives.

INVITE A MEMBER OF YOUR GROUP TO READ JOHN 10:11 AGAIN.

Discuss the following:
* Who is the shepherd in this passage? Who are the sheep?
* What does verse 11 say that the shepherd does for his sheep?
* How are we like sheep? Why do we need Jesus to shepherd us through this life?

INVITE A MEMBER OF YOUR GROUP TO READ JOHN 10:12-13 AGAIN.

Discuss the following:
* **What is the difference between the hired man and the shepherd?**
* **Who does the wolf represent in this passage?**
* **What happens when the hired man sees the wolf approach?**

INVITE A MEMBER OF YOUR GROUP TO READ JOHN 10:14-15 AGAIN.

Encourage your girls to circle the "I am" statement in verse 14. Help them to see the intimacy that is expressed when it says "I know My own sheep, and they know Me."

Lead girls to think about the person that knows them the best. What are some clear evidences that someone knows us well (they can read our facial expressions, they know our favorite things, they know what to do when we are hurting, etc.). Even more intimate than the relationship we just described is the way the Lord knows us and knows what it best for us.

Discuss the following:
* **What does the shepherd do when the wolf approaches?**
* **How does this symbolize God's great love for us?**

The shepherd doesn't run or think about his own safety. A good shepherd is willing to lay down his life for the sheep. This is what Jesus did for us on the cross! He defeated the enemy and conquered death so that we might have life.

We are like sheep. Without our Good Shepherd, we have no place to turn for salvation, provision, peace, or protection from the enemy.

Challenge your girls to examine their lives as you ask the following:
* **How have you seen the Lord guide and protect you like a Shepherd?**
* **Do you follow His lead willingly or do you try to do things on your own first? Explain.**

Live it Out

Allow your girls a few minutes to consider what they have learned in this session and how it applies to their lives. Direct them to page 86 in their student books and encourage them to answer the following questions in the space provided.

* **What dangers in this life scare you? Based on what we've studied, how can you face those without fear?**
* **Are there battles you're trying to fight in your own power? What changes do you need to make?**

Once girls have recorded their answers, challenge them to follow through with any changes they listed. One way the girls will help each other follow through is by encouraging and praying for one another. Transition to the Dwell Challenge.

Dwell Challenge

Each session will conclude with a time of prayer and accountability groups.

IN THIS TOGETHER: Instruct girls to find a partner or a small group of three and share what they wrote in the *Live It Out* section on page 86 of the student book. Point them to the box called *In This Together* where they can list each other's prayer requests. They can also make notes to help encourage and hold one another accountable to follow through with anything God is leading them to live out this week.

DWELL ON THIS: Direct girls to remain with their partners/groups from the previous activity and encourage them to consider how this week's focal verse, Psalm 91:4, has impacted their lives. Invite each girl to share how God is using the truths of this verse to shape her perspective and character.

Remind girls that the Lord is our Shepherd who desires to lead, guide, and protect us daily. End this time by reading Psalm 23 to your group. Lead them to highlight this passage in their Bibles and meditate on it in the days ahead.

Close your time in prayer.

A Safe Dwelling

BECAUSE YOU HAVE MADE THE LORD—MY REFUGE,
THE MOST HIGH—YOUR DWELLING PLACE,
NO HARM WILL COME TO YOU;
NO PLAGUE WILL COME NEAR YOUR TENT.

PSALM 91:9-10

Get Started

This week focused on the significance of God's protection in light of the battles we face in this life. While it is comforting to study about God's protection, we must not miss the reality that He never promises us a life exempt from suffering and pain. This can be a difficult truth for us to reconcile at any age but especially in our younger years. Take time to let your girls wrestle with their questions as you walk through this session. As a leader, you don't have to know all the answers—there are some things that remain a mystery to us from our limited perspective. Your greatest ministry will happen as you help your girls know and trust the character of God more deeply.

Direct girls to think about their dream house. Pose the question below, then write their responses on a large sheet of paper or white board.

* **If you were building your dream house, what would be your "must haves"?**

Encourage them to give reasons behind their list. Ask which of the following was most important as they thought about "must haves" for their dream home:

* Safety
* Comfort
* Style / Appearance

Now, guide the group to discuss what precautions they would take to protect their dream house and those living in it (insurance, alarm system, smoke detectors, etc.). Ask girls if a disaster could still happen, even with all those precautions and safety measures in place. The answer is yes. The reality is that unexpected disasters can hit even the most well prepared houses and leave a lot of damage behind.

Transition: Psalm 91 talks a lot about the protection of God and how He offers us a refuge from the storms of life. Does this mean that disaster will never strike our lives or that we will never face painful circumstances? Allow your girls time to discuss this question based on what they have learned this past week. Make sure the discussion leads girls to the understanding that God is sovereign—nothing takes Him by surprise and nothing is beyond His control. God does allow suffering and disaster to strike His children, but in every circumstance, He is working all things for His glory and our good.

Talk it Out

Review the material the girls studied last week. Encourage them to share anything they highlighted in the student book or had questions about.

>>QUICK SUMMARY:
1. We can trust God's sovereignty even as we face difficult battles.
2. The glory of God and the power of His presence is worth any sacrifice on our part.
3. God's will for us often includes suffering and pain but always for a greater purpose.
4. God gives us everything we need to be victorious in battle.

Once girls have shared highlights, lead them to discuss the following questions to ensure they understand the main points for this week. These three questions are listed in the student book at the top of page 98. Every session will have a *Dwelling Together* page at the end which will be used in this group time. Encourage girls to turn to this page and follow along during the group meeting.

* If God is protecting us, why does suffering still happen?
* What spiritual resources has God given us that help us in our time of need?
* How powerful is the peace Jesus offers us? Explain.

Further Study

Because the topics of suffering and spiritual battles are such heavy ones, encourage your girls to spend a few minutes quietly praying for wisdom and understanding. When enough time has passed, close by praying for each girl by name.

Encourage girls to share about a difficult battle they have faced in the past (this could be a spiritual attack or a season of suffering). Once they have shared, ask the following questions:

* In the midst of the battle did you feel like God had left you to fight for yourself? Explain.
* Looking back now, can you see evidence that God was near and fighting for you? Explain.

Help them to see that God is with us in every battle we face. As children of God, we are never alone or forgotten. It is essential for your girls to recognize that God is in control at all times. Even in the midst of calamity. Suffering does not happen because God stopped paying attention and it slipped past Him. Suffering happens because we live in a broken world. But even our pain has purpose. Nothing is without eternal potential. Our most difficult moments offer us opportunities to trust and glorify God in profound ways.

This is a hard truth to embrace so allow your girls time to talk through this as they process. Ask for a volunteer to read the last paragraph on page 93 of the student book aloud, then discuss what it says. It is listed below for your convenience.

God promises protection and He is always true to His Word. We struggle to understand that truth because most of us have a different definition of protection. We base our understanding of protection around the idea of physical comfort and safety in the moment. God's definition covers our physical, emotional, and spiritual well-being for all eternity.

INVITE A MEMBER OF YOUR GROUP TO READ <u>ROMANS 8:31–39</u>.

Discuss the following:
  * **What does this passage tell us about the love and faithfulness of God?**
  * **How does this passage highlight the protective nature of God?**
  * **What or who can separate us from His love?**
  * **How can we experience victory and peace in the midst of our battles?**
  * **How should we respond to the truth of these verses?**

This is a beautiful and comforting passage for all who belong to the Lord. Because God is for us, we can rest in His victory. Because God has justified us, no accusation can stand against us. Because God has rescued us, nothing can ever separate us from His love. God desires for us to draw near to Him in our pain and let the power of His presence bring us peace. Our suffering is temporary; healing and wholeness in Christ is eternal.

Challenge your girls to examine their lives as you ask the following:
  * **Do you believe God can use your pain for an eternal purpose? Explain.**
  * **Do you cling to the peace of God when suffering comes or do you run to other sources for comfort? Explain.**

Live it Out

Allow your girls a few minutes to consider what they have learned in this session and how it applies to their lives. Direct them to page 98 in their student books and encourage them to answer the following questions in the space provided.

* **How do you handle suffering when it directly impacts your life? Do you need to change the way you view suffering based on what we've studied?**
* **How can you bring glory to God when facing difficult circumstances?**

Once girls have recorded their answers, challenge them to follow through with any changes they listed. One way the girls will help each other follow through is by encouraging and praying for one another. Transition to the Dwell Challenge.

Dwell Challenge

Each session will conclude with a time of prayer and accountability groups.

IN THIS TOGETHER: Instruct girls to find a partner or a small group of three and share what they wrote in the *Live It Out* section on page 98 of the student book. Point them to the box called *In This Together* where they can list each other's prayer requests. They can also make notes to help encourage and hold one another accountable to follow through with anything God is leading them to live out this week.

DWELL ON THIS: Direct girls to remain with their partners/groups from the previous activity and encourage them to consider how this week's focal verses, Psalm 91:9-10, have impacted their lives. Invite each girl to share how God is using the truths of these verses to shape her perspective and character.

Close your time in prayer.

The Promise

WHEN HE CALLS OUT TO ME, I WILL ANSWER HIM;
I WILL BE WITH HIM IN TROUBLE.
I WILL RESCUE HIM AND GIVE HIM HONOR.
I WILL SATISFY HIM WITH A LONG LIFE
AND SHOW HIM MY SALVATION.

PSALM 91:15-16

Get Started

You made it! Way to go! Thank you for being faithful to lead and invest in the lives of your girls. We hope this final gathering will be a sweet time for your group.

Sometimes the tendency for the last week of a study is to rush through or combine with another session. We would encourage you to be faithful to the content of this week's material. Looking at the promise of eternity in the presence of our Savior is the best way we could possibly end this study.

Before the session, gather eight sheets of paper in various colors (or pretty sheets of scrapbook paper) and write the title of each session on these sheets: *Made to Dwell, Dwelling Distractions, Dwelling in Community, Dwelling Delights, Your Dwelling Place, Faithful Protector, A Safe Dwelling, The Promise.* Bring additional colored/scrapbook paper and markers for everyone in your group. Instruct girls to take a sheet and write their names at the top. Guide them to fill up the rest of the paper with descriptions of what they have learned over the course of this study—encourage them to use sentences, bullet points, or illustrations as they reflect on lessons learned. Display the session title sheets you created as a reference for the girls while they work.

Transition: Allow girls time to share their work. Affirm them as they share and encourage them to continue in the coming weeks to reflect on and put into practice what God has been teaching them. For a final visual, instruct the girls to place all the sheets on the floor (including the eight title sheets) and connect them in one large square or rectangle using clear tape. Remind girls of the quilt example given on page 105 of the student book. Just like God's grace is woven into our individual stories, the Lord desires for our lives as believers to be woven together in community. Invite girls to share what they have learned from each other or how they have been encouraged by one another throughout this study. Challenge them to stay connected beyond this gathering and continue experiencing the kind of biblical community the Lord has called them to.

Talk it Out

Review the material the girls studied last week. Encourage them to share anything they highlighted in the student book or had questions about.

>>QUICK SUMMARY:

1   God is faithful and trustworthy. He will keep His promises.
2   As believers, we are compelled to call out to God through prayer.
3   God will satisfy our souls here on earth and throughout eternity.
4   If we trust the promises of Psalm 91, our lives should reflect the hope we have in Christ.

Once girls have shared highlights, lead them to discuss the following questions to ensure they understand the main points for this week. These three questions are listed in the student book at the top of page 110. Every session will have a *Dwelling Together* page at the end which will be used in this group time. Encourage girls to turn to this page and follow along during the group meeting.

* **What are the promises given in Psalm 91:14-16?**
* **How does this passage describe the one who receives God's promises?**
* **What does Psalm 91 as a whole teach us about the character of God?**

Further Study

We will focus on two main points in this session: Promises of God and Hope of Eternity.

1. Promises of God

INVITE ONE OF YOUR GIRLS TO READ ALL OF <u>PSALM 91</u> ALOUD FOR THE GROUP.

We have seen a number of promises throughout Psalm 91 (a few examples include protection, refuge, deliverance, peace, justice, spiritual resources, honor, salvation, and satisfaction for our souls). Lead girls to share personal examples of how they have experienced any of these promises of God in their lifetime.

Discuss the following:
* **Which of the promises found in Psalm 91 is most difficult for you to believe is true in your own life? Why?**

At times, we may struggle to believe that God's protection is real for us or that His deliverance is true in our current circumstances. We may look at our lives and wonder if His peace is a future reality and not a promise we can experience today. Living in this broken world is challenging. Unwavering hope can only be found by trusting in the faithfulness of God's character and believing in the certainty of His promises.

2. Hope of Eternity

INVITE A MEMBER OF YOUR GROUP TO READ 1 PETER 1:3-9.

Discuss the following:
* **What is the source of our hope?**
* **What is Peter referring to when he talks about an inheritance kept in heaven for us?**
* **What good can come as a result of our various trials?**
* **What is the ultimate goal of our faith?**

INVITE A MEMBER OF YOUR GROUP TO READ TITUS 1:1-2.

Discuss the following:
* **What hope does Paul use to build us up in verse 2?**
* **What aspect of God's character does Paul point to as evidence that this hope will be fulfilled?**

Challenge your girls to really examine their lives as you ask the following:
* **How does the hope of eternity impact the way you see your circumstances right now?**
* **Based on how you live, what would those closest to you say is your source of hope? Explain.**

For those who place their trust in the redemptive work of Christ for salvation, the hope of eternity is a sure reality. We can experience joy and peace through every circumstance because we know we will spend forever in the glorious presence of Jesus!

Live it Out

Allow your girls a few minutes to consider what they have learned in this session and how it applies to their lives. Direct them to page 110 in their student books and encourage them to answer the following questions in the space provided.

✳ **Do you trust God to keep His promises? How does that shape the way you live? Explain.**
✳ **Is your prayer life vibrant and consistent? How has learning to dwell in the presence of God affected your prayer life?**

Once girls have recorded their answers, challenge them to follow through with any changes they listed. One way the girls will help each other follow through is by encouraging and praying for one another. Transition to the Dwell Challenge.

Dwell Challenge

Each session will conclude with a time of prayer and accountability groups.

IN THIS TOGETHER: Instruct girls to find a partner or a small group of three and share what they wrote in the *Live It Out* section on page 110 of the student book. Point them to the box called *In This Together* where they can list each other's prayer requests. They can also make notes to help encourage and hold one another accountable to follow through with anything God is leading them to live out this week.

DWELL ON THIS: Direct girls to remain with their partners/groups from the previous activity and encourage them to consider how this week's focal verses, Psalm 91:15-16, have impacted their lives. Invite each girl to share how God is using the truths of these verses to shape her perspective and character.

Close this last session by praying the words of Ephesians 3:14-21 as a parting challenge. These are precious words of affirmation and hope in the One who desires to accomplish immeasurably more than all we could ask or imagine.

*Notes

*Notes